c. b. eady

twenty days & nights

poems from an ordinary life

table of contents

day one : reflections on nature 1
night one : the 99 2
day two : reflections on nature 4
night two : prairie reverie 5
day three : reflections on family 6
night three : tiny haiku 7
day four : reflections on time 8
night four : sleeping pills 9
day five : reflections on dating 10
night five : trains 11
day six: why 12
night six: morning 13
day seven : they sky 14
night seven : sixth toe 15
day eight : feminist musings 16
night eight : a stone for sam 18
day nine : not a fragile flower 19
night nine : spring 20
day ten : groceries 22
night ten: becoming 23
day eleven : david 24
night eleven : date 25
day twelve : waiting 26
night twelve : perfect murder 27
day thirteen : the dishwasher 28

night thirteen : crucible 29
day fourteen : dylan 30
night fourteen : tounges 31
day fifteen : how we fell 32
night fifteen : canary 33
day sixteen : missing 34
night sixteen : forty-one 35
night seventeen : revival 37
night eighteen : support 38
day twenty : old friend 39

thank you for reading these poems
they must be for you

day one : reflections on nature

she doesn't care if we are alive or dead
it is all the same to her
if we are fed or the worms are fed

everything dies
we are all born
we all hunger

we should care
it's possible
we don't

night one : the 99

cold to the bone
shivering

jeans are a bad choice for rain

once you get wet
you are damp
until june

the 99 is always full

rain
makes its way
into your shoes

before you finally
catch a break
and catch a bus

packed in
with the moist
dog smell

you drip
drip drip drip

day two : reflections on nature

a scatter of wildflowers
encroaches on
charcoaled stumps

mushrooms only grow here
where the forest fell

the earth scorched
red beneath the black

night two : prairie reverie

the heat
last month Martha lost another calf
the corn wasn't coming in fast enough
the irrigators being levied by the province
"just you wait, Norm,
someone better build an ark!"
Norah said
always the optimist

The churchgoers
lined up
for lemonade

"the Good Lord knows
it's too late for those sinners!"
Norah guffawed,
tapping
the cover
of her bible
with her
fat thumb

day three : reflections on family

I loved your sharp angles
your soft edges
your warm centre
until I realized
I was a visitor

transient

standing with blue fingers
splayed out
trying
to absorb
some heat

night three : tiny haiku

your gentle heart beats
against the delicate ear
of our sleeping son

day four : reflections on time

get up brush teeth make breakfast cold cereal and
milk toast and jam feed the cat dress Henry where's
Raechel did she come home last night make coffee
make lunch have a shower get dressed which shoes
your socks don't match kiss and clip the kid into
the car seat start stop drop Henry at daycare battle
traffic battle traffic battle traffic no parking find
parking find caffeine eat something do coursework
prep for class listen watch study take notes
participate tire drift find caffeine remember where
I parked fight traffic fight traffic fight traffic pick
up Henry kiss and clip the kid into the carseat start
fight traffic make dinner bathe the kid feed the cat
open the mail review homework kiss Henry put
him to bed hi Raechel required readings answer
emails where's your dad got to fall asleep

night four : sleeping pills

one for you
one for me
gotta get this girl to sleep

your mamma don't care
that your daddy ain't there
and that you didn't have a thing to eat

day five : reflections on dating

don't date boys
who call girls cunts

you are what they call you
at least to them you are
so if they call you
beautiful baby hot stuff

they are never really calling "you"
they are performing a summoning

bitch slut whore
you are just a blank canvas
to them

luckily they lack the discipline of magic

so you can be
whoever
the fuck
you want

night five : trains

Henry hoozle
loves his woozle
Tigger wants to eat it
no matter if we put it up
where he cannot quite see it

Tigger wants
to scratch the couch
and chew upon his basket
Henry says
he mustn't eat the train
because it's plastic

day six : why

because the alarm wasn't set
because you have the time
because I wanted to be something
because we had to replace the fucking roof
because you are impatient with us
because I am tired of my neck aching when I roll
over
because this is going to cost us a hundred thousand
dollars
because teenagers are hard and toddlers are harder
because the cat was paralyzed by the fall and needs
physiotherapy five times a day
because I ache to love you the way my sixteen-year-
old self loved but I don't remember how

night six : morning

the night is relentless
it plods on
no matter how hard
we try to slow it down
the morning mocks us
the sun is gray
I worry
it does not wish us well

day seven : they sky

the sky was infinitely far above us
clear through to space
lying on my back I thought I would fall

it has grown closer
lowering until
we have to walk with our heads down
to avoid cracking them on the hard blue

crushing us slowly
with out noses flat against the concrete
until we cannot look up

night seven : sixth toe

mon cheri

mon grand erreur

I can only count to dix au francais

or douze

if I count on my toes

day eight : feminist musings

my feminist sisters might crucify me
I do not think we should be sending women to war
though we are competent killers

I thought feminism
and pacifism
were on the same side

I thought we might stop
sending our fathers
husbands
brothers
sons to be killed
by someone else's father
husband
son
or brother
and never
send our mothers
sisters
wives

or daughters
into the belly of wolves
in the name of Dianna
or crown and country or
balance or
profit or
good sportspersonship
and instead live in peaceful demonstration
against the atrocities of violence
against women
men
children
cultures
and races
in the name of love
peace
and feminism

night eight : a stone for sam

too high to fly

you dropped
like a rock

(and stopped)

day nine : not a fragile flower

more of the cactus variety
really
then an orchid or petunia

comfortable in arid climates
and not too concerned with drawing blood

happy then
to be sharp and
somewhat succulent

night nine : spring

with the laying on of hands
I give you
everything I can
a tupence worth
of affection
and pomegranate juice
with which
to wash
the winter down

oh fair one
oh fond one
oh lady bright
oh strong one

I would heal us
if I could
I would recite incantations to dark goddesses
I would light candles and gather flowers
I would breathe your name in like your perfume
I would lay my hands over your womb

I would touch your hair
I would whisper ancient things
out under my breath
and bring forth spring

with the laying on of hands
I give you
something fragrant
and warm

day ten : groceries

eggs
gluten-free noodles
oranges
apples (not the green kind)
play time with my son
mushrooms
butter
a letter to my lover
spelt flour (?)
turmeric
kosher salt
dinner with my daughter
green seedless grapes
fresh medjoul dates
if they have any
otherwise the dried ones are fine

night ten : becoming

I am sinking into stone
my heart is

stone is
becoming
my image

my eyes
cannot see
through lids
heavier
than wings

day eleven : david

did you believe in mercy
if used sparingly
it can last months
or at least until it goes bad
and all of the idealists rise
to the top
and start growing martyrs like mould

night eleven : date

I am patient
and eager
but more
than a little
forgetful

I was wondering (?)
if you want to go
dancing maybe

or if you'd rather
stay
home
that's good too

especially when
it's raining

day twelve : waiting

I am waiting
always waiting
for the shower
for a phone call
for the bus
for a paycheque
for that feeling
always waiting
always patient
and quiet
and waiting
and waiting
and waiting
for something else
for someone else
for a reason
to motor on
and find something
to do

night twelve : perfect murder

I have planned the perfect murder
I will conspire with time
and feed you only
the fattiest medium rare beef

and when you go
I will tell them
everything

I will tell them
that you were not
evil
you were just
wrong

day thirteen : the dishwasher

funny how it seems
we can't write
when we need to write
(what we need to write)
that the internal censor
is on and
working overtime

and you just wanna
punch out

so you go
to pay the bill
and find
only change
in your pockets

night thirteen : crucible

throw my heart
into a crucible
and you will find
when the fat burns away,
equal parts of
love and animosity

day fourteen : dylan

add drugs to the shopping list
keep us all sane
test the water and find out
what it's laced with

goodnight goodnight

can you hear what it sounds like
when a heart breaks

the dog is dead
sleep tight sleep tight

live only with the monsters
we can laugh at
or not at all
but don't let them see light

if you must
sedate them
and put them to bed

night fourteen : tounges

I have been speaking to you
in more than one language
I have been hearing the tongues
of my ancestors
wag and bitch
and pacify
and accuse
always a little
disappointed

day fifteen : how we fell

in the beginning
we were sent spinning
like tops
we collided
exchanging energy
(equals ehm-ce squared)
as force
and creating gravity
with the shear mass
and velocity
of our attraction
(the inevitable consequences
may be inertia but
I prefer to remain optimistic
and pretend that
a drag coefficient
cannot exist

in space)

night fifteen : canary

america
our hearts

a small bird
lives inside my ribcage

you are so afraid
we are so afraid

the future only holds
uncertainty

or rather
a deadly certainty
nobel laureates or not

soon there will be
no birds left
to sing our stories

day sixteen : missing

samantha samantha
your ashes are cold
though your eyes
in my memory shine

I keep waiting
and praying
for the grief to grow old
so that I can get on with my life

scatter these ashes
to the sea to the sea
and stand
at the prow of the boat

then bury our memories
silently silently
scatter these ashes
to the sea

night sixteen : forty-one

at 16
it was passion, anguish
sorrow necessary

at 18
it was fiction imaginary
pretended performed

at 23
it was lost hidden
invisible vapour

at 27
it was possible painful
wanted but wasteful

at 35
it was promised yearned for
formalized celebrated

at 41
it is complicated complacent
tried troubled

at 55
will it will be easier

night seventeen : revival

take the beating heart from my chest and place it in
your breast
take the air from my lips and breathe again
borrow my pieces
borrow some time
I still can't figure out which parts of me are mine
and which are yours
for the taking

night eighteen : support

your wide mouth
obscene and animal

you have ruined me so often

there are numbers coursing through my veins
my heart can count them
one two
three four
five six
seven eight

do you know how to count
when it matters

night nineteen : 40 years

in 40 years
my children
may have children
of their own
trying to eek a living
on a planet
turned to bone

day twenty : old friend

everyday

I betray myself to you

a bit more

and soon

you will know me so well

you'll wonder

how my simplicity could have hidden

for so long

behind these everyday betrayals

of myself

CPSIA information can be obtained
at www.ICGtesting.com
Printed in the USA
LVOW13s1932080917
547978LV00012B/56/P